WOULD YOU RATHER...

be the smartest kid in your school but get nothing for Easter

or

be the dumbest kid but get all the candy in town?

tube down a chocolate river

or

go swimming in a pool full of peeps?

your parents wear bunny
suits on Easter

or

sing Easter songs to
you all day long?

have crazy, rainbow hair for
Easter

or

have to ride to school
in your parent's crazy,
rainbow car?

WOULD YOU RATHER...

wake up on Easter with rabbit legs

or

dinosaur arms?

be in charge of planning the town Easter egg hunt

or

leading the town easter parade

It rain candy on Easter

or

have the power to make it rain on people you don't like on Easter?

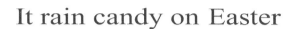

Participate in an Easter egg hunt

or

an Easter egg throwing fight, like the people living in the country of Bulgaria?

WOULD YOU RATHER...

wake up each morning to find
a basket of candy

●————————————— or —————————————●

have a talking pet bunny?

go to school dressed as the
Easter Bunny

●————————————— or —————————————●

dressed in fancy, but itchy
Easter clothes?

wake up Easter morning to find your backyard full of rabbits

or

baby ducks?

wear an Easter bonnet

or

an Easter basket on your head?

decorate your house
with Easter lilies

or

Christmas poinsettias?

eat carrot cake

or

hot cross buns, a spiced
sweet bun made with fruit?

win the golden prize egg at
your Easter Egg hunt

or

get a 3-foot tall chocolate
Easter rabbit in your basket?

leave a nice note

or

play a funny, sneaky trick
on the Easter Bunny?

WOULD YOU RATHER...

eat a meal of cooked
mushy carrots

●————————— or —————————●

black licorice jelly beans?

have a hot spring day

●————————— or —————————●

a snowy blizzard?

WOULD YOU RATHER...

get 10 eggs with
money in them

or

30 eggs filled
with candy?

Go to an Easter party
with lots of
baby animals to snuggle

or

an Easter party with
water balloons to throw?

WOULD YOU RATHER...

it rained on Easter and
you had to hunt eggs inside

or

its a beautiful sunny day,
but your chocolate eggs
melt?

eat Peeps

or

Bunny Corn (like candy corn)
everyday for breakfast
for a week?

have to sleep on itchy Easter grass

or

take a bath in pink Easter egg dye?

eat jelly beans that taste like banana pudding

or

Ice cream sundaes?

WOULD YOU RATHER...

catch winter snowflakes

or

spring raindrops
on your tongue?

spend the day hanging out
with the Easter Bunny

or

Santa Claus?

WOULD YOU RATHER...

drink chocolate milk

or

milk flavored
like jelly beans?

have a giant pet lamb

or

a giant pet bunny?

WOULD YOU RATHER...

wear rain galoshes

or

duck feet with
your Easter outfit?

get a chocolate
Easter bunny

or

a chocolate Easter bilby (a little
marsupial with giant ears) like kids
in Australia get in their baskets?

have eggs that are hard to find, but full of your favorite candy

or

eggs that are easy to find but full of candy thats just ok?

have bunny ears

or

a cotton tail?

WOULD YOU RATHER...

participate in a deviled
egg eating contest

•———————— or ————————•

a hot dog eating contest?

swim in a pool of
Easter egg dye

•———————— or ————————•

a pool of caramel sauce?

WOULD YOU RATHER...

wear a colorful clown wig

or

a wig made out
of Easter grass?

find the egg that is the
hardest to find

or

find the most eggs?

WOULD YOU RATHER...

have to spend the day
waddling like a duck

or

hopping like a bunny?

stay clean and
dry on easter

or

partake in squirt gun and
water wars drenching
others with water as is
tradition in Poland?

WOULD YOU RATHER...

eat candy that tastes
a little like carrots

_____ or _____

carrots that
taste like candy?

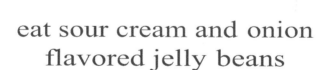

eat sour cream and onion
flavored jelly beans

_____ or _____

BBQ chip flavored
jelly beans?

21

get a huge basket filled with
candy but only 10 eggs to find

or

a tiny Easter basket
but 50 eggs to find?

wear your swimming suit

or

your pajamas to
church on Easter?

WOULD YOU RATHER...

eat a fruity dessert

—— or ——

a chocolatey dessert
for your Easter treat?

get a sunburn
from playing outside

—— or ——

blisters from
shoveling snow?

23

have to eat last
years stale Easter candy

or

only get Peeps in
your Easter basket?

celebrate spring by flying
a kite and playing outside

or

by celebrating Maslenitsa, or
"Pancake Week" a Russian folk
holiday meaning that winter is
ending?

WOULD YOU RATHER...

be famous for eating
the most jelly beans

or

the most marshmallows?

be a butterfly

or

a honey bee for the day?

hunt Easter eggs in the morning

or

have a nighttime egg hunt?

eat root beer flavored jelly beans

or

lemonade flavored jelly beans?

WOULD YOU RATHER...

dye eggs with colored dyes

or

decorate them with
paint and stickers?

meet the Easter Bunny

or

travel to the end
of a rainbow?

splash in a mud puddle

or

get caught out
in a rainstorm?

someone surprised you
with a handful of M&Ms

or

sour gummy bunnies?

WOULD YOU RATHER...

stay home for Spring break
but get an epic Easter basket

or

travel somewhere fun but
not get an Easter basket?

fall face first into
a spring mud puddle

or

have to sing a song in front of
the whole school?

WOULD YOU RATHER...

capture one of
Santa's reindeer

or

the Easter Bunny?

plant a garden of fruits and
vegetables

or

beautiful flowers?

go for a bike ride

or

fly a kite on a Spring day?

go to school dressed
like the Easter Bunny

or

a leprechaun?

hunt Easter eggs that you dyed and decorated

or

plastic eggs?

be the leader of the Easter parade

or

ride on the float with the Easter Bunny?

WOULD YOU RATHER...

receive chocolate covered ants

or

chocolate covered grasshoppers in your Easter basket?

crack open a chocolate egg to find it filled with Jello

or

vanilla pudding?

WOULD YOU RATHER...

have cute bunny ears

or

webbed duck feet?

eat jelly beans that
taste like frog legs

or

rotten eggs?

34

wake up and find you've been covered in marshmallow fluff

or

caramel sauce?

crack open a mysterious Easter egg and release a dragon

or

a unicorn?

WOULD YOU RATHER...

have a map knowing
where all the Easter
eggs are hidden

or

enjoy having all
the eggs be a surprise?

find $100 in an Easter egg

or

a ticket to Disney World?

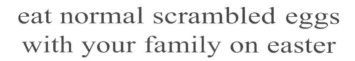

eat normal scrambled eggs
with your family on easter

or

get together with your whole town
for an omelette made of over 4500
eggs like the people of Haux, France
do for their Easter celebration?

your parents drive you to
school in a Bunny-mobile

or

walk you in to school
dressed like a giant bunny?

have Easter ham

or

Easter tacos for lunch
after hunting eggs?

be the star of a terrible
Easter movie

or

have a small part in
a really great movie?

WOULD YOU RATHER...

live in a nest
with baby birds

or

live in a burrow
with baby bunnies?

spend Easter with your
favorite movie character

or

your favorite TV character?

WOULD YOU RATHER...

spend Easter in a bakery
surrounded by desserts

•—————— or ——————•

in a pizza shop?

have to dress up like the
Easter Bunny and entertain
a party of little kids

•—————— or ——————•

clean out the rabbit
cages at the zoo?

WOULD YOU RATHER...

go watch an Easter parade

or

see a cart of exploding fire-
works to celebrate Easter
like they do in Florence, Italy?

hunt Easter eggs
in Antartica

or

the Sahara Desert?

WOULD YOU RATHER...

go mini-golfing

or

do an Easter egg roll,
like they do each year
at the White House?

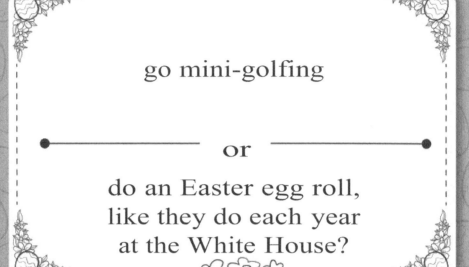

baby chicks had
rainbow feathers

or

baby bunnies had tie-dye fur?

WOULD YOU RATHER...

everyday be Easter

•——————— or ———————•

your birthday?

only get rotten carrots in
your Easter basket

•——————— or ———————•

have only carrots to eat all
day on Easter?

WOULD YOU RATHER...

have an assortment
of pastel dyed Easter eggs

— or —

red eggs only like they do
in Greece to represent the
color of life?

Easter was canceled
all over the world because
of something you did

— or —

just canceled for your
family?

WOULD YOU RATHER...

have to cook Easter dinner

or

have to clean up after your family's Easter party?

get buried in a pile of marshmallow peeps

or

a pile of skittles?

WOULD YOU RATHER...

crack open an egg to find
a baby dinosaur

— or —

a troll with rainbow hair?

eat ham for Easter lunch

— or —

iguana and turtles like
some people in
the country of Columbia?

be a talking caterpillar

or

a beautiful butterfly?

have a traditional
Easter egg hunt

or

dress up like Easter witches
and beg for chocolate eggs
which is what kids do in
Scandinavian countries?

WOULD YOU RATHER...

your dog ate your very
important homework

or

your Easter basket?

get your Easter story
published in the newspaper

or

star in a cheesy Easter
commercial?

WOULD YOU RATHER...

hunt Easter eggs

or

Easter bunnies like the people of Otago, New Zealand who have an annual bunny hunt every Easter to rid farmland of excess bunny populations?

be able to put a curse on someone so they only get bad candy in their Easter basket

or

be able to cast a spell on your own basket so you get everything you want?

WOULD YOU RATHER...

your mom send out an Easter text to everyone you know, of you dressed in your pajamas

or

dressed like a bunny?

the Easter Bunny traveled on a magical unicorn

or

a super fast hover board?

Have your pants fall off
during your easter egg hunt

or

Trip and roll down a hill
and land in rabbit poop?

go back to school

or

play Would You Rather
games all day?

Made in the USA
Monee, IL
03 April 2023

31175774R00028